IDENTIFYING

BUGS AND BEETLES

The new compact study guide and identifier

IDENTIFYING

i

BUGS AND
BEETLES

The new compact study guide and identifier

Ken Preston-Mafham

CHARTWELL
BOOKS, INC.

A QUINTET BOOK

Published by Chartwell Books
A Division of Book Sales, Inc.
114, Northfield Avenue
Edison, New Jersey 08837

This edition produced for sale in the U.S.A., its
territories and dependencies only.

ISBN 0-7858-0877-9

This book was designed and produced by
Quintet Publishing Limited
6 Blundell Street
London N7 9BH

Creative Director: Richard Dewing
Art Director: Clare Reynolds
Designer: Michael Head
Project Editor: Doreen Palamartschuk
Editor: Rosie Hankin
Illustrator: Tony Oliver

Typeset in Great Britain by
Central Southern Typesetters, Eastbourne
Manufactured in Singapore
by Bright Arts Pte Ltd
Printed in Singapore
by Star Standard Industries Pte Ltd

All photography, except jacket, reproduced by
permission of Jean Preston-Mafham, Ken Preston-
Mafham, Mark Preston-Mafham, and Dr. Rod Preston-
Mafham for Premaphotos Wildlife. Jacket photography
reproduced by permission of Martin P. Land,
N. V. Vassilev, and John Feltwell for Wildlife Matters.

CONTENTS

INTRODUCTION

Bugs and beetles can be found in every type of habitat, from gardens, parks, and woodlands to mountaintops and in lakes, ponds, and rivers. With their tough drought-resistant exteriors beetles are particularly well adapted to the hot arid conditions in deserts, where they are often the most abundant insects. Many species of both bugs and beetles are serious pests in gardens and on farmland. Others, such as ladybug beetles, are beneficial to mankind because of their depredations against such serious pests as aphids and scale insects.

BUG OR BEETLE?

The first question to be answered in using this book is how to tell a bug from a beetle. With the exception of a few shiny plump beetle-like bugs, the differences are quite obvious and, with just a little experience, can be seen at a glance, as explained below.

Bugs and beetles belong to two quite distantly related groups of insects which

Two instars of the Australian shield-backed bug *Tectocoris diophthalmus*, distinguished by differences in size and coloration. The two orange nymphs have just molted. They will soon harden and change to the brilliant metallic blue.

have very different methods of developing from egg to adult. Bugs belong to the order Hemiptera, and along with such familiar insects as grasshoppers, crickets, cockroaches, and earwigs undergo an "incomplete" metamorphosis which proceeds as follows. The juvenile stages are known as nymphs, which resemble miniature versions of the adults. These nymphs slowly develop through a series of molts and instars, during each of which tiny wing-pads on the outside of the body gradually grow until, after the final molt, the fully-winged adult (in winged species) emerges. In the majority of these families the nymphs utilize the same food as the adults.

Beetles belong to the order Coleoptera, and along with such insects as butterflies, bees, and flies, are considered to be more advanced insects on account of their "complete" method of metamorphosis. The creature which emerges from the egg is known as a larva. It is quite different than the adult and, unlike in most bugs, the adult and larval beetles do not necessarily share the

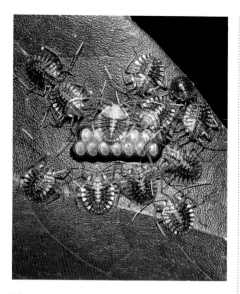

These *Edessa* sp. stink bug nymphs which have recently emerged from their eggs are just miniature versions of the adults. Their first meal will be from their own eggshells, from which they will pick up symbiotic protozoa which live in the gut. In many herbivorous bugs these play a vital role in digestion.

a suitable interval the adult finally emerges from the pupa. In beetles whose larval diet is nutritionally poor, such as many wood-boring species, entire development from egg to adult can take many years to complete.

There is no simple rule for instantly distinguishing the immature stages of bugs and beetles. Bug nymphs always have legs, while many beetle larvae lack them, especially in darkling beetles (family Tenebrionidae) and weevils (family Curculionidae). If any doubt exists, then a quick inspection of the underside will reveal that a bug nymph will always have a needle-like feeding rostrum projecting downward from its head, or folded lengthwise beneath its body. By contrast, beetle larvae have biting mouthparts in which a pair of jaws normally figures conspicuously.

same source of food. Thus, whereas a longhorn beetle larva will have developed on a diet of wood inside a tree-trunk, the adult will feed solely on nectar and pollen taken from flowers. The larva goes through a series of molts until eventually, instead of changing finally into an adult, it enters a quiescent stage called a pupa. It is inside the pupa that the incredible process of metamorphosis takes place, during which the cells comprising the larval structure are broken apart and reassembled, like a complex jigsaw puzzle, to form the adult insect. After

After crawling up a tree trunk at night, the nymph of this Australian cicada attaches its claws securely to the bark. A split then develops in the midline of the pronotum, through which the soft pallid adult gradually emerges.

Adults of the two groups can also usually be easily distinguished on this basis, but can also be told apart when seen from above and without any need for handling. In bugs, members of the suborder Homoptera, with their membranous wings held tent-like at an angle above the body, are quite unlike any beetles. In contrast, many members of the suborder Heteroptera could present problems, especially stink bugs (superfamily Pentatomoidea), which many people routinely confuse with beetles. The distinguishing feature is the way the wings meet above the back. In most stink bugs and other heteropterans the forewings, held flat against the body, meet in such a way that the membranous areas of the wing-tips overlap to form a

The larva of the tenebrionid beetle *Zophobas rugipes* is legless and very similar to that of the closely related meal-worm *Tenebrio molitor*, whose larvae are easily bred as food for various small animals.

The six-legged larva of the seven-spot ladybug *Coccinella 7-punctata* is quite unlike the black-spotted orange adult with its shiny domed body. Both adult and larva do however feed on aphids.

The pupa of the seven-spot ladybug is normally placed in full view on a leaf or stem. The molted skin of the larva is just visible on the right, at the point where the pupa is affixed to the leaf. By contrast, most beetle pupae are concealed from view.

triangle. A second triangle is normally formed by the scutellum. Bugs therefore normally have two triangles on their backs (see fig. 1).

In beetles the hardened wing-cases or elytra (actually modified front wings) meet together in a straight line down the middle of the back (see fig. 2). In most beetles the elytra are held upward out of the way so that the folded hindwings can be unfurled for flight. After landing, the hindwings are neatly folded away and the elytra closed. In the very beetle-like shield-backed bug (Scutelleridae) there is no line down the middle of the back where the wing-cases meet, thus indicating that it is not a beetle.

An adult leaf-footed bug (Coreidae) showing its stiletto-like sucking mouthparts (rostrum).

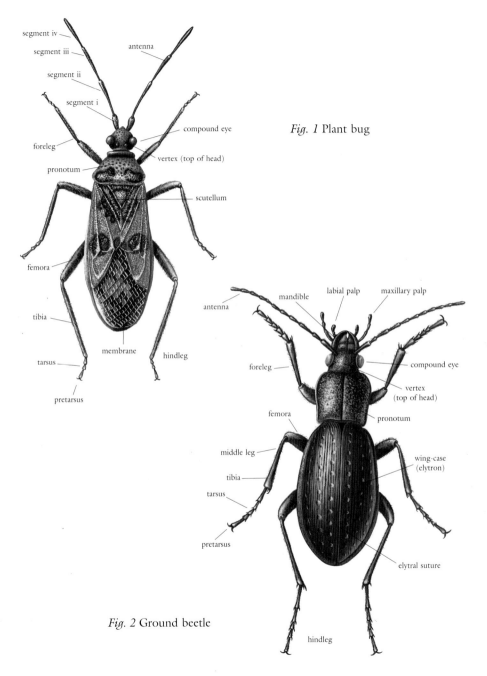

Fig. 1 Plant bug

Fig. 2 Ground beetle

HOW TO USE THIS BOOK

The first step is to decide whether or not you are dealing with a bug or a beetle, using figs. 1 and 2, in conjunction with the introduction. Then go through the photographs until you find the insect which closely matches the one you want to name. The information included within the "family" heading should then be consulted, along with the description of the insect you have chosen, to see whether or not your identification is likely to be correct.

The family tree below shows how the species are listed in order of classification, using their Latin and common names. We have selected three example species, the Anchor stink bug, the Peanut bug, and the Bee Beetle to show how the classification system works.

Kingdom – Animalia
(All animals)
|
Phylum – Arthropoda
(All animals having jointed legs)
|
Class – Insecta
(Insects)

Order – Hemiptera (Bugs)		*Order – Coleoptera* (Beetles and weevils)
SUB-ORDER HETEROPTERA	SUB-ORDER HOMOPTERA	
Superfamily PENTATOMOIDEA (e.g. Shield-backed and Stink bugs)	Superfamily FULGOROIDEA (e.g. Lantern flies and Butterfly bugs)	Superfamily SCARABAEOIDEA (e.g. Stag, Hercules beetles, scarabs, and chafers)
Family Scutelleridae (Shield-backed bugs)	*Family* Fulgoridae (Lantern flies)	*Family* Scarabaeidae (Scarabs)
Genus *Stiretrus*	Genus *Laternaria*	Genus *Trichius*
Species *anchorago* (COMMON NAME Anchor stink bug)	Species *laternaria* (COMMON NAME Peanut bug)	Species *fasciatus* (COMMON NAME Bee beetle)

Note that the genus and species are written in italics whenever they occur within the normal text.

The identifier section of this book is arranged in three groups, the sub-orders Heteroptera and Homoptera, within the Order Hemiptera (Bugs), and the Order Coleoptera (Beetles and Weevils). A brief description introduces each family, and each genus representing its family is identified with its species name, common name, together with information on its general characteristics and known distribution.

The symbols accompanying each entry convey essential information at a glance.

KEY TO SYMBOLS

LARVAL STAGES

 Larvae external, feeding visibly on leaves, stems, etc.

 Larvae are concealed, e.g. in timber, on roots, etc.

HABITAT

 Open areas generally, e.g. roadsides, grasslands, scrubland, etc.

 Forest and woodland, but often mainly in more open spots.

 Common in gardens and backyards.

 Mainly in deserts.

In or beside water.

FOOD

 Herbivore, feeding on plants, e.g. leaves, stems, sap, wood, or fungi, etc.

 Predator, feeding on other small animals and insects.

 Scavenger, using dung, corpses, etc.

 Larvae are predators, but as adults the species is herbivorous.

BUGS
Order Hemiptera

Commonly known as bugs, this order of insects contains some 67,500 described species, split into two suborders, the Heteroptera and the Homoptera. The unifying feature of all bugs is their piercing and sucking mouthparts, housed in a beak-like rostrum.

SUBORDER HETEROPTERA

Known as the **true bugs** (to avoid confusion with inaccurate term "bugs" used to describe any insect-like creature), the members of this suborder possess a "hinged" rostrum which can be swung downward and forward from its stowed position along the underside of the body. The wings (if present) are held flat across the back when not in use, and the forewings exhibit a substantial hardened portion.

Superfamily **ARADOIDEA**

BARK BUGS, FLAT BUGS *Family Aradidae*

This is a medium-size family of some 1,800 species of very flattened bugs which usually live on or under the bark of trees, mainly those infected by fungi upon which the bark bugs feed. A few species make use of sap rather than fungi. Body size ranges from ⅛ to ½ inch, while the head is very characteristic in that the antennae stem from tubercle-like outgrowths.

DYSODIUS LUNATUS

COMMON NAME Bark bug

DESCRIPTION With a body length of about ½ inch this is one of the largest of the bark bugs. It often forms large aggregations on fallen trees in the American tropics. Note the very flattened body and the series of projections along the sides, that mimick a piece of flaking bark. Species from the USA and Europe are generally similar, though the latter are very much smaller.

DISTRIBUTION American tropical zones; common in rainforest in Costa Rica.

Superfamily CIMICOIDEA

DAMSEL BUGS *Family Nabidae*

Damsel bugs are quite slender dull-coloured insects which prowl slowly about among vegetation or on the ground, searching for small insects or spiders on which to prey. Just under 400 species are known worldwide, all being predators. During mating, the male penetrates the female's body-wall and the sperm makes its way through her body fluids toward the ovaries. Three species of *Nabis* in North America help control the boll worm *Heleothis zea*, a major pest.

DOLICHONABIS LIMBATUS

COMMON NAME Heath damsel bug

DESCRIPTION The body length ⅓–½-inch makes this a typical member of the family, although difficult to distinguish from other related species without reference to minute details of the body structure. It is found among the rank grass of damp meadows and in dense low vegetation bordering marshes. The adults are present from early July onward and are only rarely fully-winged. As with all damsel bugs, it will tackle any prey small enough to subdue. This one is feeding on a birch shieldbug nymph.

DISTRIBUTION Common throughout Europe, including the British Isles; many similar-looking species in North America.

Superfamily **PENTATOMOIDEA**

TORTOISE STINK BUGS *Family Plataspidae*

With their very rotund shiny bodies and flat undersides the members of this family may easily be mistaken for beetles. The scutellum is very large, enclosing most of the abdomen, but there is no line down the middle of the back, unlike in beetles. About 500 species have been described, chiefly from the warmer regions of the world. Most kinds feed on plants, but a few species make use of fungi.

LIBYASPIS COCCINELLOIDES

COMMON NAME Tortoise stink bug

DESCRIPTION In common with many members of the family, this species exhibits a marked difference between the adult and juvenile stages. The matte-finish nymphs are well-camouflaged against the bark of their host tree, while the ¾-inch long adults stand out and are very shiny and quite brightly colored. Note how the head of the adults is completely concealed beneath the huge pronotum.

DISTRIBUTION Tropical Africa and the island of Madagascar.

SHIELD-BACKED BUGS
Family Scutelleridae

The 400 or so members of this family are often mistaken for beetles. The scutellum is very large and extends across the entire abdomen, but without the beetle-like line down the middle of the back. Many species are brilliantly colored in metallic shades. All members of the family feed on plants and some have attained pest status.

STIRETRUS ANCHORAGO

COMMON NAME Anchor stink bug

DESCRIPTION The anchor-like marking is less obvious on the color-form pictured than on the equally common black and red form. This ⅓–½-inch long bug is a predator, feeding mainly on the soft-bodied larvae of various insects, but also on adult beetles as pictured. It mainly inhabits woodlands.

DISTRIBUTION USA and Central America.

TECTOCORIS DIOPHTHALMUS

COMMON NAME Harlequin bug

DESCRIPTION Males of this conspicuous bug attain a length of ¾ inch, while females may reach ⅞ inch. The scutellum is bright orange, patterned with scattered patches of iridescent blackish-blue or green. It feeds on various members of the hibiscus family, including cotton, on which it can become a pest. The female stands guard over her egg batch but does not stay with her offspring.

DISTRIBUTION Tropical and sub-tropical eastern Australia.

STINK BUGS
Family Pentatomidae

This is by far the largest family of stink bugs, with over 5,000 species worldwide. Most species have a rounded or broadly oval outline, although pointed projections on the sides of the pronotum are frequent. Sound production is quite common, being achieved by rubbing a row of pegs on the back legs against a ridged area on the underside of the abdomen. The great majority of pentatomids suck plant sap, but some common species are predatory. Odorous defensive secretions give rise to the common name.

ACANTHOSOMA HAEMORRHOIDALE

COMMON NAME Hawthorn shield bug

DESCRIPTION The berries of hawthorn trees (*Crataegus* sp.) form the principal food for both adults and nymphs, whose red and green coloration blends in well with the foodplant. The adults first appear in August and September, and then reappear in the following spring after hibernating through the winter. The body length of about ½ inch readily distinguishes it from the similar birch shield bug (*Elasmostethus interstinctus*) which is slightly smaller.

DISTRIBUTION Common and widespread in Europe, including the British Isles.

ELASMUCHA GRISEA

COMMON NAME Parent bug

DESCRIPTION The rather small female (about ⅓ inch) stands guard over her diamond-shaped egg-mass, usually laid on leaves, for around 2–3 weeks until the nymphs emerge. She then stands on sentry duty upon or beside her developing offspring for the next few weeks, until they are almost ready to molt into adults. The nymphs are much more colorful than the rather somber adult.

DISTRIBUTION Common on birch trees in Europe, including the British Isles.

GRAPHOSOMA ITALICUM

COMMON NAME Minstrel bug

DESCRIPTION With its longitudinal black and red stripes this ½-inch long bug can be mistaken for no other European species save *G. semipunctatum*, in which the pronotal stripes dissolve into dots. As will be obvious from the picture, the adults are quite different than the nymphs, which are a camouflaged shade of grayish-cream. The main foodplants are various umbellifers (carrot family).

DISTRIBUTION South and Central Europe, excluding the British Isles.

PALOMENA PRASINA

COMMON NAME Green shield bug

DESCRIPTION This is one of many similar-looking green shield bugs, but the only one present in the British Isles or common in northern Europe. The adults reach a length of ½ inch, feeding on a huge variety of plants, often in gardens. The slightly bigger green vegetable bug (*Nezara viridula*) is similar, but narrower in outline. It is common in warmer parts of the world, including southern Europe, the USA, and Australia, and has a striking pink, green, and black nymph.

DISTRIBUTION Found throughout many parts of Europe.

PERILLUS BIOCULATUS

COMMON NAME Eyed stink bug

DESCRIPTION As can be seen from this mating pair, the color of this striking bug is very variable. The markings can be red, orange, yellow, or white, but always set against a black background. This ⅓–½-inch long species is an important predator of the Colorado potato beetle.

DISTRIBUTION Widespread throughout most of the USA.

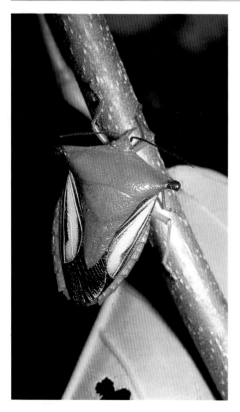

PEROMATUS sp.

COMMON NAME Banana bugs

DESCRIPTION This is one of two genera of large handsome stink bugs found in the American tropics, the other being *Edessa*. The adults reach a length of 1 inch or more, and are often boldly striped on the underside in black and yellow. The sides of the pronotum usually bear blunt projections. Many species feed on poisonous plants of the potato family *(Solanaceae)* and are occasionally introduced into some cooler regions of the world on shipments of tropical fruit, especially bananas.

DISTRIBUTION American tropical zones.

Superfamily **LYGAEOIDEA**

SEED BUGS *Family Lygaeidae*

This is a large worldwide family, with over 3,000 described species. The adult bugs are generally rather elongate-oval in outline, and the antennae project from low down on the head, below the eyes, When wings are present, five veins are clearly visible in the membranous hindmost portion of the front wings; many species have forms with vestigial wings. The rostrum consists of four segments. Some giants of the family reach a length of nearly ⅞ inch, but most are much smaller. The great majority of species feed on plants, but a few attack the eggs or immature stages of small insects or mites, while a few suck blood.

ONCOPELTUS FASCIATUS

COMMON NAME Large milkweed bug

DESCRIPTION Both the boldly marked ⅓-inch long black and orange adults and the bright red nymphs often congregate on milkweed plants, whose seeds comprise the main food. Particularly large overwintering groups can sometimes be seen on mild winter days.

DISTRIBUTION Eastern United States and Central America.

LYGAEUS KALMII

COMMON NAME Small milkweed bug

DESCRIPTION This handsome ⅓-inch long bug is red and black with a red mark on top of the head and two white spots on the wings. It is found on the flower heads and seed pods of various milkweeds. Two common European species are similar: *Lygaeus equestris* also has white spots on the wings, whereas *L. saxatilis* lacks them.

DISTRIBUTION Most of North America and down into Mexico.

NEACORYPHUS BICRUCIS

COMMON NAME Ragwort seed bug

DESCRIPTION At only ¼–⅓-inch this is rather smaller than the other common red and black seed bugs already mentioned. There is a conspicuous white cross on its back. It feeds solely on yellow-flowered ragworts such as *Senecio anonymus*. It can be difficult to find a lone bug, with mated pairs being the norm. This is because the males hang on to their mates in order to guard them against rivals until the next batch of eggs is laid, a daily event.

DISTRIBUTION Widely spread in eastern North America.

Superfamily **PYRRHOCOROIDEA**

COTTON STAINERS *Family Pyrrhocoridae*

This is a family of more than 300 species of bugs mainly found in the warmer parts of the world. Most species are warningly colored in red and black, especially in the nymphal stages, the adults often being rather drabber. The triangular head bears a long slender four-segmented rostrum, allied to four-segmented antennae.

DYSDERCUS sp.

COMMON NAME Cotton stainer bugs

DESCRIPTION This mating pair of just under ½-inch long cotton stainers in Mexico is representative of this large worldwide group of very similar-looking bugs. Even with expert knowledge it can be difficult to separate one species from another. The bright colors exhibited by both adults and nymphs warn that the bugs are unpleasant-tasting. The formation of large feeding aggregations of adults and nymphs is a common feature, with some species being pests of cultivated plants, including cotton.

DISTRIBUTION Mexico and southwestern regions of the USA.

PYRRHOCORIS APTERUS

COMMON NAME Firebug

DESCRIPTION The adults of this brightly colored ⅜-inch long bug are very seldom fully winged, usually occuring as short-winged. Its all-black head distinguishes it readily from various common red and black species of *Lygaeus*. After winter hibernation the adults often form huge conspicuous swarms on the ground. The firebug feeds on the seeds of a variety of plants, most especially members of the mallow and hibiscus families (Malvaceae).

DISTRIBUTION Much of Europe, especially in the south, extending to the Middle East. Very rare in the British Isles.

THICK-HEADED BUGS
Family Largidae

The 100 or so members of this family are very closely related to the Pyrrhocoridae, in which they are still placed by some experts. Largids mainly suck sap, but a few species are predacious. The family is heavily concentrated in the warmer parts of the world, where some species can reach 2 inches in length.

ARHAPE CICINDELOIDES

COMMON NAME Largid bug

DESCRIPTION This black and white ⅜-inch long species from the deserts of the south-western United States is one of a number of largids which spend their lives among detritus on the ground. It rather resembles some of the tiger beetles with which it lives, hence the specific name, but it is more properly considered as an excellent mimic of some of the common black and white velvet ants (mutillid wasps) which pack a powerful sting.

DISTRIBUTION Deserts of southwestern USA and Mexico.

Superfamily **COREOIDEA**

LEAF-FOOTED BUGS *Family Coreidae*

The members of this family are sometimes known as squash bugs because one American species is a pest of cultivated squash. However, the rest of the 2,000-odd species feed on a wide variety of plants. The adults are invariably fully winged, and the membranous portion of the front wings bears a characteristic array of parallel veins. The four-segmented antennae are narrowed where they join the head. Some species attain a length of 1¾ inches, while many are brightly colored as nymphs but molt into drab brown or black adults. Stink glands are well developed.

NARNIA SNOWI

COMMON NAME Snow's leaf-footed bug

DESCRIPTION This rather small ⅓-inch long narrow-bodied species belongs to a genus typical of the deserts of the southwestern United States and Mexico. Here many of the commonest species feed on the fruits and stems of cacti. The species pictured feeds on a variety of plants, including yucca flowers (pictured) and juniper berries. Note the enlarged and flattened hind legs of this male, typical of the family. Most members of this genus are rather drably colored in grays and browns.

DISTRIBUTION Deserts of southwestern USA and Mexico.

ACANTHOCEPHALA TERMINALIS

COMMON NAME Common leaf-footed bug

DESCRIPTION The hind tibiae of this ⅜–⅞-inch long bug are expanded and leaf-like, unlike in the rather similar-looking true squash bug (*Anasa tristis*) which has cylindrical hind tibiae. The leaf-footed bugs feed on a wide variety of plants, and there are many broadly similar species.

DISTRIBUTION Over much of the USA and down into Mexico.

BROAD-HEADED BUGS
Family Alydidae

Once included with the Coreidae, the alydids are now widely treated as a separate family, being much more slender-bodied and elongate than the average coreid. The head is noticeably broad, much more so than in coreids, being more than half the width of the rear margin of the pronotum. The fourth antennal segment is always slightly curved and considerably longer than the previous segment. The nymphs of many species mimic ants. Just under 300 species are known from around the world.

HYALYMENUS sp.

COMMON NAME Ant bug

DESCRIPTION The ½-inch long adult pictured is typical of most alydids found in far distant parts of the globe. Note the enlarged and spiny back legs, typical of the genus, and slender build. The rostrum has been swung downward, ready to suck on the green fruit on which the bug's front legs are resting. The nymph is an excellent mimic of a large ant.

DISTRIBUTION Widely distributed in the warmer zones of the Americas. Similar-looking genera are found from Europe eastward to Australia and down into Africa.

SCENTLESS PLANT BUGS
Family Rhopalidae

All the known species of this 150-strong worldwide family feed on plants, sucking the seeds of a broad range of herbaceous kinds. In so doing, a few species make a nuisance of themselves and become pests. The body is often decorated with surface dimples, spines, and hairs. Some people still treat this family as part of the Coreidae.

LEPTOCORIS TRIVITTATUS

COMMON NAME Boxelder bug

DESCRIPTION The narrow brick-red markings down both sides of this ⅜–¾-inch long bug are characteristic. It is found in deciduous woodlands and in gardens, often on leaves of boxelder and other maples. However, it is also common on many other types of trees and shrubs, feeding on flowers and fruits. *L. rubrolineatus* from west of the Rockies is similar.

DISTRIBUTION Eastern North America.

CORIZUS HYOSCYAMI

COMMON NAME Red-backed bug

DESCRIPTION The superficial resemblance of this ⅓-inch long bug to some similar-size common black and red seed bugs can be confusing. However, this species is noticeably hairy and there are numerous veins in the forewing membrane (lygaeids never exceed five). The adults are usually found singly, sitting around on various plants. Adults which have survived the winter can be seen in June and July, with the new generation of adults appearing in late September.

DISTRIBUTION Widespread in Europe; rare in the British Isles.

Superfamily TINGOIDEA

LACE BUGS *Family Tingidae*

Tingids are mainly very small, flattened insects, with the largest being only ⅛ inch in length. Only under the microscope can the full beauty of the lace-like structure of the adults be appreciated. There are more than 1,800 species worldwide, all feeding on plants, with some becoming pests. A few species induce the formation of swellings, or galls, on their foodplants.

GARGAPHIA SOLANI

COMMON NAME Eggplant lace bug

DESCRIPTION This is one of several similar-looking species which are specialists on certain foodplants. The preferred foodplant of the eggplant lacebug is horsenettle (*Solanum carolinense*), but it also utilizes many other members of the potato family (Solanaceae). The females guard their own offspring, as well as those of other females who "dump" their eggs for others to foster. The adult guarding this mass of nymphs is at top-right of the picture.

DISTRIBUTION Widespread in North America.

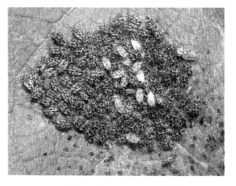

Superfamily **MIROIDEA**

PLANT BUGS *Family Miridae*

With 7,000–8,000 described species from around the world, this is by far the biggest of all the families of heteropteran bugs. Mirids are lightly built rather small bugs, the largest reaching ¾ inch in length. Antennae and rostrum are both four-segmented, while winged varieties exhibit two closed cells in the membranous region of the front wings. Although most species feed on plants, some are predatory and of value in controlling pests. Most bizarre are the select band which specializes in stealing prey from spiders' webs.

CALOCORIS STYSI

COMMON NAME Mirid bug

DESCRIPTION With a length of ¼–⅓ inch this is very much an average kind of mirid in size, but not in color, being one of the prettiest mirids in Europe. The yellow markings are diagnostic and cannot be confused with any other species. The eggs are laid in crevices in tree bark, and the resulting larvae eventually become adult in mid-June after feeding on a wide variety of plants, but especially on the developing catkins of stinging nettle *Urtica dioica*. Soft-bodied insects such as aphids also form part of the diet.

DISTRIBUTION Common throughout Europe, including the British Isles.

Superfamily **REDUVOIDEA**

AMBUSH BUGS *Family Phymatidae*

Often treated as a subfamily within the Reduviidae, the 100-odd known species of ambush bugs cannot be confused with any other heteropteran. Although usually quite small (about ⅕ inch), the body is bizarre in appearance, often being extravagantly decorated with flaps and other outgrowths from the sides. The front legs are highly modified for a raptorial lifestyle – they seize prey with their legs – forming a gin-trap much like the front legs of a praying mantis.

PHYMATA EROSA

COMMON NAME Common ambush bug

DESCRIPTION Like other ambush bugs, this species lies in wait on flowers to trap unwary insects in its spiny front legs. These are clearly visible in the above illustration of a mating pair, which were well camouflaged and almost invisible on the flowers they had chosen. The bug responds with lightning speed to the approach of a potential meal. The European species *P. monstrosa* and *P. crassipes* look very similar.

DISTRIBUTION Several similar-looking species over much of North America and Mexico.

ASSASSIN BUGS
Family Reduviidae

Over 5,000 species are known from this worldwide family of largely predacious bugs. A few species suck blood and in so doing may affect man and domestic animals. Body length varies from ⅓–1⅝ inches, while shape varies from short and relatively stout to long and almost thread-like. The head is very narrow, while the rostrum has three segments.

APIOMERUS FLAVIVENTRIS

COMMON NAME Bee assassin bug

DESCRIPTION Numerous similar-looking species of this genus wait in ambush on flowers in North America. Sometimes the bug is a good color-match for the flower, but this does not seem to be necessary in order to catch prey, as seen here with a bug having caught a bee on a contrasting yellow flower. Reduviids are bold predators, ready to tackle large fierce prey. The rostrum injects a powerful fast-acting toxin which invites care in handling, as the effect on a human finger can be more painful than a bee or wasp sting.

DISTRIBUTION Western North America and Mexico, with many similar-looking species.

PSELLIOPUS ZEBRA

COMMON NAME Zebra assassin bug

DESCRIPTION As in most species of *Pselliopus*, the legs, antennae, and abdomen of this ½-inch long bug are banded in black and creamy white. These bugs are found sitting or walking on foliage, rather than on flowers. They prey on a wide variety of small insects and spiders. *P. cinctus* from the eastern USA differs mainly in having a plain brownish-red top to the pronotum.

DISTRIBUTION Mexico.

Superfamily **GERROIDEA**

WATER STRIDERS or POND SKATERS *Family Gerridae*

Members of this family are conspicuous elements of the surface life of ponds, lakes, and rivers, and even the open ocean, certain gerrids being the only insects to effect successful colonization of this environment. The 500-odd known species are found throughout the world, the majority being wingless, although winged forms do arise when overcrowding forces a move to new waters. Gerrids move easily over the surface film on their middle and hind legs, which are long and slender and have unwettable feet. The body is also furnished with a dense felt of unwettable hairs.

GERRIS LACUSTRIS

COMMON NAME Common pond skater

DESCRIPTION With a length of ⅛–⅜ inch, this is an average member of the family, with the drab appearance typical of the group. In common with all gerrids, it can detect stranded prey struggling on the water surface, using a combination of acute eyesight and ripple-sensitive hairs on the body and legs. Thus, several gerrids will quickly converge on a floundering damselfly. Cannibalism also occurs, especially toward young nymphs. There are many similar-looking species in North America (e.g. *G. remigis*). Here the pond skater is skating on duckweed.

DISTRIBUTION Widespread in Europe and most of Asia.

Superfamily **GELASTOCOROIDEA**

TOAD BUGS *Family Gelastocoridae*

Like their namesakes, toad bugs have a squat warty appearance and proceed via a series of hops. The very flattened face is surmounted by two large bulging eyes, while the short four-segmented antennae are normally held out of sight beneath the eyes. All the 85 or so species are predatory, and no species exceeds ½ inch in length.

GELASTOCORIS PERUENSIS

COMMON NAME Toad bug

DESCRIPTION Like most toad bugs, this brown, warty ⅓-inch long species runs around on the borders of ponds and streams and in rainforests, where it blends in well with its surroundings, resembling a small pebble. The front legs are modified for snapping up prey, comprising smaller insects. Numerous similar-looking species are found throughout the Americas e.g. the western toad bug (*G. variegatus*) from the western USA and Mexico, and the big-eyed toad bug (*G. oculatus*) from most of the USA and Mexico.

DISTRIBUTION Streamsides and ponds in tropical America.

Superfamily NOTONECTOIDEA

BACKSWIMMERS *Family Notonectidae*

Backswimmers have a rather boat-like body and strong oar-like hind legs which are fringed with hairs. These propel the insect, on its back, in a series of jerks through the water. Although aquatic, backswimmers make regular visits to the water surface, gathering air and storing it beneath the wings and on special hairs on the underside of the abdomen. More than 300 species are known worldwide.

NOTONECTA GLAUCA

COMMON NAME Common backswimmer

DESCRIPTION The bug pictured has come to the surface and is lying briefly on its back in order to gather an air supply. When it submerges, it will have to row powerfully downward, as it is now lighter than water. Like all water boatmen, it is a ferocious predator, using its powerful beak-like rostrum to stab small prey such as damselflies, small fish, and tadpoles. If carelessly handled, the result can be a very painful stab in the finger. Its length is usually about ½ inch.

DISTRIBUTION Many similar-looking species around the world. Commonest North American species is *N. undulata*.

SUBORDER HOMOPTERA

This suborder differs from the Heteroptera in the following ways. The rostrum or beak cannot be directed forward to feed and the wings are held tent-like above the body when at rest. More than 42,500 species are known, many of which produce honeydew as a waste product.

Superfamily FULGOROIDEA

LANTERN FLIES *Family Fulgoridae*

This family of about 750 species contains some of the world's most bizarre looking insects, especially in the shape of the head, which is often modified in all kinds of strange ways. There are no really small species, the smallest being ⅜ inch in length, while the largest can reach 4 inches or more. The family reaches its maximum diversity in the tropics, especially in rainforest areas.

LATERNARIA LATERNARIA

COMMON NAME Peanut bug

DESCRIPTION This spectacular bug is one of the giants of the family, reaching a length of 3⅛ inches with a wing-span of 4 inches. The common name is derived from the huge bulbous projection on the head which resembles an unshelled peanut. This head was once erroneously thought to be luminous, hence the common name of lantern flies given to the whole family. The peanut bug sucks the sap from the trunks of large trees, and when disturbed opens its wings to reveal intimidating eyespots.

DISTRIBUTION Over much of the American tropics and subtropics.

BUTTERFLY BUGS
Family Flatidae

The common name given to these bugs is derived from some of the larger and very colorful tropical species, which resemble butterflies when in flight. More than 1,000 species are found around the world, mainly in tropical and subtropical zones. The broad front wings are never transparent and have blunt ends, being held at a steep angle above the body when at rest.

PHROMNIA ROSEA

COMMON NAME Flower-spike bug

DESCRIPTION Both the adults, which are about ⅞ inch long, and the strange white nymphs form large feeding groups on the branches of small trees. The adult bug can be either vibrant pink or green, and when assembled the mass of bugs bears a remarkable resemblance to an attractive spike of brightly colored flowers. The nymphs have long waxy white "tails," a distinctive and common feature in the family.

DISTRIBUTION Tropical Africa and the island of Madagascar.

FALSE LANTERN FLIES
Family Dictyopharidae

Although widely distributed around the world, this family only contains some 500–600 species of mostly green or brown bugs. The head is prolonged forward in a long snout-like projection called the cephalic horn. This rather resembles the head of some smaller lantern flies, hence the common name. Most species feed on grasses.

EPIPTERA EUROPAEA

COMMON NAME European lantern fly

DESCRIPTION This bright green ⅜-inch long bug is found on a broad range of herbaceous plants, particularly umbellifers (carrot and parsley family). The adults can be found from the end of June through October, often only singly. The complex network of veins toward the tips of the transparent wings is diagnostic. In central Asia this species can be a problem in melon plantations. The common name is misleading, as this bug is not a member of the Fulgoridae.

DISTRIBUTION Europe eastwards to central Asia; absent from the British Isles.

Superfamily **CERCOPOIDEA**

FROGHOPPERS *Family Cercopidae*

With over 2,500 species mainly around warmer zones of the world, these bugs are usually brown, able to jump, and have a frog-like appearance. The front wings are longer than the body and the tibiae are round in cross-section. They feed on plant sap.

CERCOPIS VULNERATA

COMMON NAME Black and red froghopper

DESCRIPTION One of the few colorful members of the family. The ⅜-inch long adults are conspicuously present from late April to June, sitting around on a wide variety of herbaceous vegetation. The nymphs form feeding aggregations on the roots of grasses, surrounded by a ball of sticky froth. Several similar species are present in Europe.

DISTRIBUTION Widespread in Europe, including the British Isles.

PHILAENUS SPUMARIUS

COMMON NAME Meadow spittlebug

DESCRIPTION In this species the nymph makes its presence far more obvious than the adult. Sap excreted from the feeding nymph's rear end forms a froth which covers its soft delicate body. The ¼-inch long adult occurs in numerous color-forms in shades of brown, black, and gray.

DISTRIBUTION Widespread in Europe, including the British Isles, and Asia; eastern and western fringes of North America.

Superfamily CICADOIDEA

CICADAS *Family Cicadidae*

In most warmer parts of the world cicadas are the most obvious of all homopterans, due to the considerable volume of noise made by the calling males. There are some 2,250 described species, ranging from a little under ⅜ inch to giants over 4 inches long. The wide blunt head is distinctive, as are the large usually transparent wings, which make cicadas strong fliers. Most species are brown, gray, green, or blackish, but some tropical kinds are beautifully colored.

TIBICEN CANICULARIS

COMMON NAME Dogday harvestfly

DESCRIPTION This 1–1⅛ inch long species inhabits coniferous and mixed woods, appearing on the wing from late summer to early fall. The nymphs live below ground, sucking the roots of pine trees, taking three years to reach the adult state. The adults emerge synchronously so that locally trees and bushes will be almost covered in them.

Males "sing" by rapidly clicking in and out a tymbal membrane, amplified by air sacs within the body, producing a sound like a circular saw cutting through timber.

DISTRIBUTION Northeastern USA and adjacent region of Canada.

Superfamily **CICADELLOIDEA**

LEAFHOPPERS *Family Cicadellidae*

This is a huge worldwide family with over 20,000 species, making it far and away the largest family within the Hemiptera. They are slender-bodied insects with a noticeable taper toward the rear end. Most species measure less than ¾ inch from head to wingtip, and even the tropical "giants" do not go much over ⅞ inch. The hind tibiae are distinctive with their angular and rather flattened cross-section, adorned with rows of spines. Leafhoppers suck plant sap, with few if any plant species escaping their attentions.

CICADELLA VIRIDIS

COMMON NAME Green leafhopper

DESCRIPTION Adults of this species are usually shades of brown, green, or yellow, although the males are often a distinct bluish shade. Females reach ⅓ inch in length, the males only just over ¼ inch. They occur from July to September on vegetation in marshy areas, where the eggs are laid in the leaves and stems of rushes. The vampire leafhoppers (*Draeculacephala*

sp.) found all over North America have larger and more pointed heads, but are otherwise similar. The rather bigger redbanded leafhopper (*Graphocephala coccinea*), from the eastern USA, is similar but has longitudinal red striping.

DISTRIBUTION Widespread in Europe, including the British Isles.

Superfamily **MEMBRACOIDEA**

TREEHOPPERS *Family Membracidae*

This is a large worldwide family containing nearly 2,500 species. Small size is normal, with about ¾ inch being the maximum body length, but numerous species form conspicuously large aggregations, both as adults and nymphs. The distinguishing feature to look out for is the considerable extension of the pronotum, which in many tropical species assumes complex and bizarre shapes.

CYPHONIA CLAVATA

COMMON NAME Ant treehopper

DESCRIPTION This ⅓-inch long treehopper is one of a number of species from the American tropics with pronotal adornments, thought possibly to be mimicking an open-jawed ant. As few predators feed on ants, this would be a reliable form of protection. The transparent wings enable the green body to blend into the leaf, strengthening the ant-like appearance. This species occurs singly as adults on low vegetation on forest edges.

DISTRIBUTION American tropics.

UMBONIA CRASSICORNIS

COMMON NAME Horned treehopper

DESCRIPTION The smaller bug (⅜ inch) with the elongate vertical blackish extension to the pronotum is this species. Facing it is an adult of *Umbonia spinosa*, with a shorter pronontal "thorn." Neither species actually mimics thorns, and seldom if ever lives on thorny trees. Both species are warningly colored, with the thorn-like projection making them difficult to swallow, giving their bad-tasting properties time to invoke rejection before any harm is done.

DISTRIBUTION Widely spread in the American tropics and subtropics, with *U. crassicornis* just getting into Florida.

Superfamily **APHIDOIDEA**

APHIDS *Family Aphididae*

Other common names for this large family of more than 4,000 species of tiny bugs are greenfly, blackfly, and plantlice. The giants among aphids only reach a body length of ¼ inch, while some species are only about ½₀-inch long. The most distinctive structural feature is a pair of tube-like cornicles or siphunculi which arise from the the fifth or sixth abdominal segments. These cornicles produce defensive secretions which entrap enemies, such as parasitic wasps. Many species have generations which alternate on different foodplants.

MACROSIPHUM ALBIFRONS

COMMON NAME Lupin aphid

DESCRIPTION Unlike some of its close relatives, the lupin aphid does not alternate its hostplant, but sticks solely to various lupins. This gray-green mealy-looking, farinacious species can be a major pest of cultivated lupins, especially in Europe where it is of recent introduction. The plump female at top right is just giving virgin birth (known as parthenogenesis) to a live nymph, the normal method of aphid reproduction in summer. In the fall, aphids mate and lay normal eggs.

DISTRIBUTION Virtually worldwide where lupins are cultivated or native.

Superfamily **COCCOIDEA**

MEALY BUGS *Family Pseudococcidae*

There are more than 1,000 species in this family distributed worldwide. Many of them are serious pests of cultivated plants and are difficult to control with chemicals. This is partly because many species have a waxy coating which often gives good protection against chemical attack. Body length is generally less than ⅕ inch. Reproduction in many species is parthenogenetic, and males are not known.

PSEUDOCOCCUS AFFINIS

COMMON NAME Glasshouse mealybug

DESCRIPTION This worldwide pest of cultivated plants in glasshouses has the waxy-white appearance typical of the group and from which the common name is derived. Like in all mealybugs, the female is wingless, but is able to walk considerable distances to colonize new plants. The female's egg-sac is abundantly covered in white waxy filaments and covers her body.

DISTRIBUTION Worldwide in glasshouses.

BEETLES
Order Coleoptera

The Coleoptera is the largest order of insects with well over 300,000 known species. The front wings or elytra are tough and horny and in most species cover the entire abdomen. The membranous hindwings (when present) are neatly folded beneath the elytra when not in use. The mouthparts are normally of the biting type, rather than adapted for sucking as in bugs.

Superfamily **CARABOIDEA**

TIGER BEETLES and GROUND BEETLES *Family Carabidae*

This is a huge worldwide family of mainly shiny predatory beetles which are usually fast and agile runners on the ground. All kinds of prey are taken, but some species are specialists on certain types. The jaws are powerful and efficient, while the antennae are slender and usually have eleven segments. Some species can reach a length of 3 inches.

CARABUS VIOLACEUS

COMMON NAME Violet ground beetle

DESCRIPTION Only in certain lights is the violet shimmer visible on the elytra of this common beetle. It varies between ⅞ and 1⅜ inch and the very smooth shiny elytra help separate it from related species which have grooved or pock-marked elytra (e.g. the European ground beetle (*C. nemoralis*) which is also common in the USA and Canada). The violet ground beetle is found in many habitats, including gardens, but is seldom seen in daytime, emerging at night to hunt slugs and other prey.

DISTRIBUTION Common over much of Europe, including the British Isles, eastwards to Siberia and Japan.

CICINDELA SEDECIMPUNCTATA

COMMON NAME 16-spot tiger beetle

DESCRIPTION This ½-inch long species is one of a group of tiger beetles from the USA in which individual species are differentiated by their varying number of spots. Tiger beetles are active on warm sunny days, running rapidly across bare open ground on their long legs. They tear prey apart with their powerful curved mandibles.

DISTRIBUTION Southwestern USA.

CICINDELA SEXGUTTATA

COMMON NAME 6-spotted green tiger beetle

DESCRIPTION The body, antennae, and legs of this ½-inch long species are a scintillating shade of bluish green. The number of white spots is variable, there often being only 3–4, or sometimes none at all. It is one of only a few tiger beetles which live in forests, where it can be found running on paths or in open areas.

DISTRIBUTION Eastern USA and adjacent areas of Nova Scotia.

CICINDELA LANGI

COMMON NAME Lang's tiger beetle

DESCRIPTION This ¾-inch long beetle is one of 90 or so members of the genus found in the USA. Most of the species, including this one, are found in the west, being characteristic insects of flat sandy areas in deserts. Tiger beetle larvae are strange creatures with huge heads which are used to block a vertical burrow. When an insect strays close, the waiting larva grabs it.

DISTRIBUTION Southwestern USA.

Superfamily STAPHYLINOIDEA

BURYING BEETLES or CARRION BEETLES *Family Silphidae*

Also called undertaker beetles, this family of over 2,000 species is widely distributed, especially across the temperate zones of the northern hemisphere. The antennae are characteristically club-shaped or have a thickened button-like tip; the hind part of the abdomen is exposed. Not all species live on carrion; some are predators, while others live on vegetable debris or fungi.

NICROPHORUS VESPILLO

COMMON NAME Burying beetle

DESCRIPTION This is one of several similar-looking burying beetles having orange bands on the black elytra. The terminal antennal segments are reddish-brown (black in the very similar *N. vespilloides*); body length is ½–⅞ inch. All members of the genus exhibit advanced parental care, burying small corpses for use as a food store in the rearing of their larvae. Male and female often cooperate in this domestic task, and communicate with their offspring through chirps.

DISTRIBUTION Found throughout the whole of temperate Europe and Asia, and across most of North America.

ROVE BEETLES
Family Staphylinidae

This comprises a huge worldwide family of beetles with over 20,000 known species. In general they are easily recognized by their very short elytra, usually much shorter than the body. However, a few species have fairly long elytra, while members of some other unrelated families also have the elytra much abbreviated. Most rove beetles are predators.

ONTHOLESTES TESSELLATUS

COMMON NAME Tessellated rove beetle

DESCRIPTION The body of this ½–¾-inch long species is liberally sprinkled with short golden hairs, which make the beetle scintillate as it moves in its characteristic jerky fashion. It can be found, often in large aggregations, on fresh dung and carrion, in which the eggs are laid. The gold-and-brown rove beetle (*O. cingulatus*) from across the whole of North America is very similar.

DISTRIBUTION Common throughout Europe, including the British Isles, and eastward into Asia.

Superfamily **CANTHAROIDEA**

NET-WINGED BEETLES *Family Lycidae*

Lycids are noticeably flattened beetles, usually with very narrow beak-like heads and robust many-segmented antennae. The rather soft pliable wing-cases are decorated with a conspicuous lattice-work of veins. In some species the mouthparts are modified to form a nectar-sucking proboscis. The larvae mostly live in rotting wood where they prey on other insects. Distribution is worldwide, with a bias towards the warmer areas.

LYCUS ARIZONICUS

COMMON NAME Arizona net-winged beetle

DESCRIPTION The ½-inch long species pictured is very similar to members of the genus found in many parts of the world. All lycids deploy distasteful defensive fluids. Beetles of many other families, plus a few moths, mimic lycids, making it important to make a careful inspection of any beetle thought to belong to this family. The end-band netwing (*Calopteron terminale*) is very similar. It is found throughout North America, but lacks the long "snout" found in species of *Lycus*.

DISTRIBUTION Southwestern regions of the USA and Mexico.

GLOWWORMS or FIREFLIES
Family Lampyridae

Some 2,000 species are found throughout the world, especially in the tropics. After dark winged males fly in search of the stationary wingless often larva-like females, flashing a light which acts as a sexual message to the females. Many females can respond with their own luminous reply. The light is produced chemically.

LAMPYRIS NOCTILUCA

COMMON NAME Common glowworm

DESCRIPTION The adult male, a ½-inch long flattened and rather narrow-bodied brown insect is seldom seen. He is not luminous, but flies around at night looking for the greenish light emitted from the rear underside of the brown larva-like females. Most often seen are the orange-spotted larvae (pictured), which may be found under stones or logs, or walking around among grass. They feed mainly on snails.

DISTRIBUTION common in central and southern Europe, including England.

SOLDIER BEETLES
Family Cantharidae

Cantharids are rather small narrow-bodied beetles with unusually soft elytra. They derive their name from the bright colors of some species, which can resemble military uniforms. The adults are generally predatory, searching for prey on flowers, but they also eat nectar and pollen. Many species are warningly colored. The larvae hunt mainly on the ground.

CANTHARIS RUSTICA

COMMON NAME Black and red soldier beetle

DESCRIPTION This ⅓–½-inch long species is one of more than 15 similar-looking species found in Europe. It is common on foliage in early summer, and is often found mating, a process which can be very protracted. The downy leather-wing *(Podabrus tomentosus)* looks very similar; it is common over the whole of North America.

DISTRIBUTION Widespread in Europe.

SOFT-WINGED FLOWER BEETLES
Family Melyridae

These generally rather small beetles resemble small soldier beetles with similarly soft elytra but much more tapered rear ends. However, the relationship between the two families is not close. The adults are generally covered with long hairs or scales, and are mainly found on flowers. The larvae are predatory, mostly living in rotten wood.

MALACHIUS BIPUSTULATUS

COMMON NAME 2-spotted flower beetle

DESCRIPTION This ¼-inch long species is easily recognized by its combination of small size and green elytra, marked with red only at their tips. It is usually seen during May and June on flowering grasses, where it spends a considerable time feeding on the pollen. The males have yellowish outgrowths called excitators on the antennae, on which the female feeds during courtship.

DISTRIBUTION Common over much of Europe, including the British Isles.

Superfamily CUCUJOIDEA

FLAT BARK BEETLES *Family Cucujidae*

Members of this family can be easily recognized by their very flattened, rather elongate parallel-sided body, although a few species are not noticeably flattened. They are usually found walking around on logs in shady forests, or can be located by searching under loose bark. Most species feed on mites and small insects, while a few can be pests of stored products such as grain.

HECTARTHRUM GIGAS

COMMON NAME Flat bark beetle

DESCRIPTION This ½–¾-inch long species can be found on damp fungus-ridden logs in many African forests. The jaws are noticeable from above, while the antennae, which resemble a string of beads, are very characteristic. The red flat bark beetle species (*Cucujus clavipes*) is distinguished by its shorter, broader pronotum and all-red body. It is found throughout North America.

DISTRIBUTION East and Central Africa.

FUNGUS BEETLES
Family Erotylidae

With their generally rather domed shiny bodies, fungus beetles could be easily mistaken for certain kinds of leaf beetles. The clubbed antennae arise in front of or between the eyes, while the feet terminate in broad, hairy pads. Erotylids feed on fungi both as larvae and adults, and some tropical species pupate in huge aggregations on fungus-infected logs in rainforests. At least one species exhibits advanced parental care.

MEGALODACNE HEROS

COMMON NAME Pleasing fungus beetle

DESCRIPTION The bright colors of this ½-inch long beetle are certainly pleasing, hence the common name. It is usually found in deciduous forests, where the females may be located laying their eggs in a fungus-infected tree.

DISTRIBUTION Forests of eastern USA.

HANDSOME FUNGUS BEETLES
Family Endomychidae

The endomychids are exclusively small beetles which rather resemble ladybugs. However, endomychids are much flatter and have much longer antennae. The form of the pronotum is also characteristic, with two lengthwise grooves at its base. Both larvae and adults are found on fungi, decaying wood, and rotting fruit.

ENDOMYCHUS COCCINEUS

COMMON NAME Handsome fungus beetle or false ladybug

DESCRIPTION This ⅕–¼-inch long beetle greatly resembles one of the smaller species of ladybugs. The larvae are also brightly colored and feed openly on fungi and fungus-infested wood, although also occurring under the bark. The adults are seen from April to June. *E. biguttatus* from North America is very similar, but has a black pronotum.

DISTRIBUTION Widespread in Europe, including the British Isles.

LADYBUG BEETLES or LADYBIRDS
Family Coccinellidae

This is perhaps the best known and well-liked family of beetles, called ladybirds in Europe. It has some 3,400 species around the world. Ladybugs are easily recognized by their domed bodies with flattened undersides, bright colors, spots, and small head which is retracted into the pronotum.

COCCINELLA NOVEMNOTATA

COMMON NAME Nine-spotted ladybug

DESCRIPTION This ¼-inch long species is easily recognized by the nine black spots on an orange background, four spots on each elytron, and one on the scutellum. The head and thorax are black and have yellowish or whitish marks on the margins. It is found in meadows, gardens, parks, fields, and marshy places.

DISTRIBUTION Throughout North America except for the southwest.

COCCINELLA SEPTEMPUNCTATA

COMMON NAME Seven-spot ladybug

DESCRIPTION At ¼–⅓-inch long, this is one of the larger European ladybugs, and perhaps the commonest and most familiar. It is easy to count the seven black spots on the individual on the left of the illustration. The smaller ladybug on the right is a ten-spot ladybug (*C. 10-punctata*). Both species are basking in the light after emerging from winter hibernation.

DISTRIBUTION Common throughout Europe, including the British Isles; introduced into the USA and now common throughout most of the northeastern states.

ADALIA BIPUNCTATA

COMMON NAME Two-spot ladybug

DESCRIPTION Many ladybugs are notorious for the variability of their pattern, but none more so than the ⅕-inch long two-spot ladybug. The degree of variation is evident from the accompanying illustration of a mating pair. Every possible combination of red and black occurs. As in most ladybugs, both larva and adult feed on aphids.

DISTRIBUTION Europe, the British Isles, and throughout the whole of North America.

HIPPODAMIA CONVERGENS

COMMON NAME Convergent ladybug

DESCRIPTION This ¼–⅓-inch long species, like many ladybugs, shows great variation, particularly in the number of black spots. There are usually 13 spots, six on each elytron and one on the pronotum. However, their number can be reduced to two or three or even zero. The two converging white stripes on the pronotum are diagnostic. Huge overwintering aggregations in the mountain forests of the west, as seen here, are typical.

DISTRIBUTION Throughout North America.

CARDINAL BEETLES or FIRE COLORED BEETLES
Family Pyrochroidae

This is a small family of mainly reddish-brown rather flattened beetles with a superficial resemblance to some net-winged beetles (Lycidae). The antennae are often pectinate or shaped like a comb. The larvae develop under bark where they attack other insects.

PYROCHROA SERRATICORNIS

COMMON NAME Red-headed cardinal beetle

DESCRIPTION This is one of two similar-looking ½–¾-inch long species which are common in Europe. The other species *P. coccinea* is easily distinguished by its black head and brighter red coloration. Both species are commonly seen on flowers such as buttercups in May and June on the edges of woodlands or along shady lanesides.

DISTRIBUTION Found over much of Europe, including the British Isles.

FALSE BLISTER BEETLES
Family Oedemeridae

A small worldwide family of beetles which, with their slim outline, could easily be confused with soldier beetles (Cantharidae). In oedemerids the antennae are long and thin, while the rather soft elytra are strongly ribbed and often taper to a point, leaving a gap between them toward the rear. The larvae develop inside rotten wood and within the dry stems of herbaceous plants.

OEDEMERA NOBILIS

COMMON NAME Thick-legged flower beetle

DESCRIPTION This is one of several species in both *Oedemera* and *Oncomera* in which the hind femora of the male are grossly swollen. At ⅓–⅜ inch, the males are slightly larger than the normal-legged females. The adults are often abundant in June and July on flowers, and fly readily.

DISTRIBUTION Widespread but scattered over much of Europe, including the British Isles.

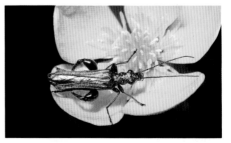

Superfamily **CLEROIDEA**

CHEQUERED BEETLES *Family Cleridae*

Some 3,000 species of these brightly colored rather hairy beetles occur around the world, although the great majority of them are in tropical areas. The larvae are normally predatory, often found feeding in the nests of bees and wasps, earning them the name of bee wolves.

TRICHODES ORNATUS

COMMON NAME Ornate chequered beetle

DESCRIPTION The elytra of this ⅕–¾-inch long beetle can be marked with red and black, as seen here, or equally commonly with yellow and black. The adults are usually found on flowers, where they feed both on the pollen and on other small insects. The larvae are found within the nests of solitary bees and wasps, where they prey upon the brood.

DISTRIBUTION Throughout the whole of North America.

Superfamily **ELATEROIDEA**

CLICK BEETLES *Family Elateridae*

The 8,000 or so species of click beetles populate a large part of the earth's land surface. Body length varies from around ⅛ inch up to 3½ inches in some tropical giants, some of which are also luminous. The body is characteristically long and rather narrow, tapering somewhat at the rear end. Some of the large tropical species are so hard that it is impossible to hammer a pin through without bending it.

CHALCOLEPIDIUS ZONATUS

COMMON NAME Harlequin click beetle

DESCRIPTION This large 2-inch long click beetle is usually found on fallen trees in forests. The margins of the pronotum bear two broad white bands, while the elytra are marked with a series of longitudinal black and white stripes. The black and white click beetle (*C. webbii*) from southwestern North America is slightly smaller (about 1½ inches) but otherwise very similar, save for its shiny black elytra on which the white is restricted to the margins.

DISTRIBUTION Widespread in South America.

SEMIOTUS AFFINIS

COMMON NAME Elegant click beetle

DESCRIPTION This is one of many large and spectacularly colored elaterids found in the tropics. The 1⅕-inch long female can often be found walking around on fallen trees on which she lays her eggs. Click beetles derive their name from the spring device on their undersides, which can propel them a few inches into the air when they are lying on their backs.

DISTRIBUTION Widespread in rainforests of the American tropics.

Superfamily **BUPRESTOIDEA**

JEWEL or **SPLENDOUR BEETLES** *Family Buprestidae*

Although there are some 15,000 species of buprestids around the world, the vast majority of them, and all the really large species, are restricted to the tropics. They are active in sunshine and have a variety of bright metallic colors. They range in size from under ⅛ inch up to 3 inches. The antennae are generally rather short. The larvae normally develop inside timber.

STIGMODERA RUFOLIMBATA

COMMON NAME 6-spotted jewel beetle

DESCRIPTION This rather small species (½ inch) can be quite common on *Melaleuca* and *Leptospermum* flowers in late spring. Note the bullet-shaped body, blunt head, antennae folded away, and scarcely visible legs, all typical features of the family. Most members of this genus are warningly colored, advertising the presence of bitter defensive chemicals called buprestins.

DISTRIBUTION Western and southern Australia, in open bushland and sandplains.

JULODIS HIRSUTA

COMMON NAME Hairy jewel beetle

DESCRIPTION This species, just over 1 inch long, is one of several abundantly hairy members of the genus occurring in southern Africa. These therefore lack the normal metallic sheen typical of the family. Various metallic species of the genus are found from the Cape region of South Africa north through Africa as far as the Middle East.

DISTRIBUTION Southern Africa, in dry areas.

Superfamily MELOOIDEA

OIL BEETLES or BLISTER BEETLES *Family Meloidae*

Most of the beetles in this family are brightly patterned in warning colors. These warn would-be enemies that the beetles should not be touched, as they can release an evil-smelling poisonous liquid from their joints when molested. The larvae are parasitic on other insects. More than 2,300 species occur worldwide, mainly in warmer areas.

CYSTEODEMUS ARMATUS

COMMON NAME Armored blister beetle

DESCRIPTION The most noticeable aspect of this desert-living beetle is its very rotund shape and tough pock-marked yellow elytra. The portly build is no accident, as this ⅜–¾-inch long species traps a ball of air beneath the elytra, which are fused, thus preventing flight. This seems to afford some protection to the body when the beetle is active in the hot sunshine of its arid environment. The all-black *C. wislizeni* is similar.

DISTRIBUTION Deserts of southwestern USA.

MYLABRIS OCULATA

COMMON NAME Eyed blister beetle

DESCRIPTION This is one of numerous brightly colored members of a widespread genus which occurs from southern Africa to Europe and tropical Asia. The adults of this species, which are just under 1 inch long, can be a pest in gardens where they eat flowers, often completely destroying them. The larvae parasitize grasshopper egg-pods beneath the ground.

DISTRIBUTION Southern Africa.

LYTTA MAGISTER

COMMON NAME Arizona blister beetle

DESCRIPTION The elytra of this ¾–1⅛-inch long beetle are bright shining black, while the head and pronotum are orange. The adults are often found eating the leaves of desert herbs and shrubs. The American Spanish fly *L. vulnerata* is similar, except for a broad black line from the center of the head backward across the pronotum. It is widespread in the west.

DISTRIBUTION Arizona.

EPICAUTA BRUNNEA

COMMON NAME Velvety blister beetle

DESCRIPTION The rather mealy-textured slim-bodied, gray adults of this species, which are about ½ inch long, are to be found in July and August on leaves or flowers in the deserts of the southwestern USA. They are most abundant after good summer rains. The larvae develop inside grasshopper egg-pods. This is the largest genus of blister beetles in the USA, with over 100 species.

DISTRIBUTION Deserts of southwestern USA.

EUPOMPHA FISSICEPS

COMMON NAME Notch-headed blister beetle

DESCRIPTION The elytra of this nearly ⅞-inch long beetle are bright shining metallic green, deeply pock-marked and fissured. The notched head is typical of the males. The larvae develop inside the nests of wild bees, while the adults eat plant tissues. There are only nine members of the genus in the USA.

DISTRIBUTION Texas and Mexico.

NEMOGNATHA LURIDA

COMMON NAME Nectar-sucking blister beetle

DESCRIPTION The ⅓–½-inch long adults are usually found on flowers in July and August. Unlike in most other beetles, the mouthparts are not adapted for biting and chewing, but are highly modified into a feeding tube for sucking up nectar.

DISTRIBUTION Western USA.

Superfamily **TENEBRIONOIDEA**

DARKLING BEETLES *Family Tenebrionidae*

Somber coloration, especially black, is the norm in this large family with its 17,000 species distributed around the globe. Most of them are small to medium-size beetles which hide away in the day and come out at night to feed, but there are numerous much larger and more attractive desert species which are mainly active in bright sunshine. The larvae develop in all manner of materials.

ELEODES LONGICOLLLIS

COMMON NAME Long-necked darkling or skunk beetle

DESCRIPTION This large ¾–1⅜-inch black beetle can be found scurrying rapidly along over the desert floor from April to September. If closely approached, it instantly stands on its head and points its rear end toward the source of danger. Thus poised, it is ready to blast an attacker in the face with a burst of noxious chemicals. More than 100 closely similar species are found throughout the USA.

DISTRIBUTION Southwestern USA and Mexico.

CTENIOPUS SULPHUREUS

COMMON NAME Sulfur dune beetle

DESCRIPTION This small ¼–⅓-inch long yellow beetle is one of a number of genera which are often included in their own family, the Alleculidae. The larvae live in the ground at the base of plants. The adults are often extremely abundant in July and August on flowers in dry sandy places, such as coastal dunes.

DISTRIBUTION Most of Europe, including the southern part of the British Isles.

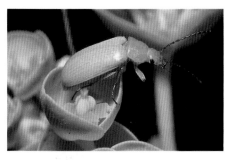

Superfamily SCARABAEOIDEA

SCARABS *Family Scarabaeidae*

This is one of the largest, most varied, and most colorful of beetle families, with more than 20,000 species around the world. The antennae bear a distinct club, consisting of several segments which can often be opened out to form a fan. This is particularly noticeable in chafers. True scarabs feed on dung, while chafers and others are herbivores and can become pests.

POLYPHYLLA DECIMLINEATA

COMMON NAME Ten-lined June beetle

DESCRIPTION This large 1–1¼-inch long chafer is easily recognized by the one short and four long white stripes on each elytron. There is a white mark on either side of the head, and three stripes on the pronotum. It is found in woodlands, where the larvae feed on the roots of woody plants. The adults are on the wing in July and August.

DISTRIBUTION Found in the Rocky Mountain areas of Canada and the USA, and in the Southwest regions.

POLYPHYLLA FULLO

COMMON NAME Pine chafer

DESCRIPTION This is the largest European chafer, with an adult length of 1–1½ inches, so therefore unmistakable by size alone, although the marbled pattern is also unique. The males stridulate loudly, and have larger antennae than the female. It occurs mainly near pine woods, where the adults feed on pine needles. The larvae eat the roots of grasses and sedges.

DISTRIBUTION Local in southern and central Europe; absent from the British Isles.

TRICHIUS FASCIATUS

COMMON NAME Bee beetle

DESCRIPTION This is one of the most distinctive and interesting of the European chafers. With its banded pattern, furry exterior, and buzzing flight it mimics a medium-size bumble bee. The ⅓–½-inch long adults are normally found on flowers, especially thistles, in June and July, chiefly in mountainous areas.

DISTRIBUTION Over most of Europe, but in the British Isles only in the north and west.

TRICHIOTINUS ASSIMILIS

COMMON NAME Flower beetle

DESCRIPTION There are eight species of the genus in the USA and Canada, all in the ⅓–½-inch size range. The adults are rather hairy, and are normally found on flowers, where they eat the pollen. The larvae develop in decaying wood.

DISTRIBUTION North America.

PLUSIOTIS GLORIOSA

COMMON NAME Striped green silversmith or glorious beetle

DESCRIPTION This striking 1–1⅛-inch long species is on the wing in July and August in the western deserts of the USA, often crashing noisily into lighted windows at night. The adults chew the leaves of junipers. Some Central American members of the genus appear to be wrought of gold, hence the name golden beetles.

DISTRIBUTION Texas to Arizona and in northern Mexico.

COTINIS MUTABILIS

COMMON NAME Green fig-eater or green June beetle

DESCRIPTION The larvae of this splendid beetle feed on roots. The 1–1⅛-inch long adults are a shiny semi-metallic green with a brownish margin to the elytra. The adults feed on many kinds of ripe fruit, and are conspicuous by their loud buzzing flight. It is a member of the subfamily Cetoniinae.

DISTRIBUTION Texas to Arizona and adjacent to Mexico.

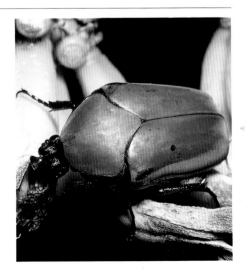

EUPOECILIA AUSTRALASIAE

COMMON NAME Splendid flower chafer

DESCRIPTION This particularly striking chafer which is nearly ⅞-inch long can be found in daytime on flowers of eucalyptus and other plants, as well as perched on leaves. The beetles chew the petals as well as eating the pollen. The hooked feet typical of chafers can be clearly seen. The larvae develop in decaying wood.

DISTRIBUTION Australia.

MELOLONTHA MELOLONTHA

COMMON NAME Cockchafer

DESCRIPTION The black pronotum of this ⅞–1½-inch long species distinguishes it from the similarly sized *M. hippocastani* and *Anoxia villosa*. All the other mainly brown European chafers are much smaller. Cockchafer adults fly chiefly around dusk, but can be found on leaves and flowers in daytime. The larvae feed on roots and can cause damage to crop and garden plants. The males have much larger antennae than the female.

DISTRIBUTION Common in Europe, including the British Isles.

ORYCTES NASICORNIS

COMMON NAME European rhinoceros beetle

DESCRIPTION With a body length of just over 1½ inches, allied to considerable bulk, this is one of the most impressive European beetles, and is on the wing in June and July. The insect pictured is a male, notable for the long horn on his head; in the female this is just a short point. The larvae are mainly found in old decaying logs. The eastern Hercules beetle *(Dynastes tityus)* from the eastern USA is similar, but gray with brownish flecks.

DISTRIBUTION South and central Europe; absent from the British Isles.

GOLOFA PIZARRO

COMMON NAME Mexican rhinoceros beetle

DESCRIPTION Like all members of this genus, the male beetle pictured has extravagantly developed horns, jutting forward from the head as well as curving upward from its top. The males use these in combination as pincers and levers to gain advantage over a rival during fights over females. Length is just over 2 inches.

DISTRIBUTION Central America.

CANTHON HUMECTUS

COMMON NAME Tumblebug

DESCRIPTION The common name is derived from the way the adult beetles tumble around as they laboriously roll a ball of dung to a nesting site. Both larvae and adults feed on such buried dung balls, often skilfully fashioned from large masses of dung. Sometimes, as in the ½-inch long beetle pictured, a single small, ready-to-use dropping is utilized. In *Canthon* the males and females cooperate to construct and stock the nest. African equivalents are mainly in the genera *Scarabaeus, Sisyphus,* and *Gymnopleurus.*

DISTRIBUTION Mexico; 18 similar species throughout the USA.

STAG BEETLES
Family Lucanidae

One of the most characteristic of all beetle families, the Lucanidae contains some 900 species of mainly large dull-colored insects in which the males have conspicuously elongated antler-like mandibles. In at least one Chilean species these equal the rest of the body in length.

LUCANUS CERVUS

COMMON NAME European stag beetle

DESCRIPTION The male has the large mandibles typical of his sex; those of the females are about one-sixth as large. The males use their mandibles in fights over females, levering one another off a tree-trunk to which the female might come to lay her eggs. Large males measure up to 3 inches long. *L. elaphus* from the northeastern USA is very similar.

DISTRIBUTION Over much of Europe, but decreasing; very local in southern England.

Superfamily CHRYSOMELOIDEA

LONGHORN BEETLES *Family Cerambycidae*

Although most common in the tropics, the 20,000 species of this large family are distributed around the world. Their main distinguishing feature is the long antennae, especially in the males, which in some species are many times the body length. The larvae generally develop in wood.

TYPOCERUS ZEBRA

COMMON NAME Zebra flower longhorn

DESCRIPTION This smallish longhorn, which measures about ⅓–½ inch, is very similar to several European *Strangalia* species. Like them, the females can be found laying their eggs in logs, tree trunks, and wooden fence and gate-posts, although the adults are most commonly found on flowers. The larvae develop in dead moist wood. There are 16 *Typocerus* species in North America, several of which differ from this one mainly in the relative amounts of yellow and black.

DISTRIBUTION Forests of eastern USA.

STRANGALIA MACULATA

COMMON NAME Spotted longhorn

DESCRIPTION This is by far the commonest of several similar-looking ½–⅞-inch long European species. Its pattern is very variable, from almost completely yellow to almost completely black. The black and yellow legs and antennae separate it reliably from similar-looking species with all-black legs and/or antennae. It is common on flowers from June through August.

DISTRIBUTION Most of Europe, including the British Isles.

JUDOLIA CERAMBYCIFORMIS

COMMON NAME Tapered longhorn

DESCRIPTION At ⅓–⅖ inch, this is like a small version of the last species, but much more chunky, with the elytra wider and shorter, and the body noticeably tapering from front to back. Large numbers of adults can be found on suitable flowers (e.g. bramble and angelica) from June through August. Several very similar species are found in Europe and across much of North America.

DISTRIBUTION Widespread in Europe, but local in the British Isles.

OCHROSTHES Z-LITTERA

COMMON NAME Z-mark longhorn

DESCRIPTION Open flowery spots in pinewoods in the Mexican high Sierras is the place to look for this small brightly colored and attractive longhorn. Body length is ⅖–⅗ inch and each elytron bears a zigzag yellow mark. The legs are yellow, except the feet which are darker.

DISTRIBUTION Mexico.

CLYTUS ARIETIS

COMMON NAME Wasp beetle

DESCRIPTION This is by far the commonest of the wasp-like longhorns in Europe. Body length is from ¼ inch in males to just over ½ inch in females, thus falling well within the range typical of wasps. The antennae are also unusually short and wasp-like, and the gait jerky. The adults are usually seen on flowers from May through July and also on sticks and dead wood where the females lay their eggs. The North American Douglas fir borer (*C. blaisdelli*) is very similar, but the bands on the elytra are pale whitish-yellow.

DISTRIBUTION Common in Europe, including the British Isles.

MONOCHAMUS OREGONENSIS

COMMON NAME Western sawyer

DESCRIPTION A rather blackish ¾–⅞-inch long beetle spotted with white flecks. Its rather long antennae are ringed with white and are about its body length. It is mainly found in conifer woods, where the larvae develop inside the timber, forming U-shaped tunnels. Several similar-looking species are found throughout North America and Europe.

DISTRIBUTION Western North America.

COSMOSALIA CHRYSOCOMA

COMMON NAME Brown flower longhorn

DESCRIPTION This is one of some 200 similar-looking North American species in several closely related genera. In all cases the tapering body (in females) is in the ⅜–⅞-inch size range; males are smaller. The elytra are normally brown and the long antennae and legs black. The adults are usually found on flowers, especially wild roses. The common and widespread *Stenocorus meridianus* from Europe is very similar in size and color.

DISTRIBUTION Western North America.

TETRAOPES FEMORATUS

COMMON NAME Milkweed longhorn

DESCRIPTION This is one of some 28 similar-looking red and black members of the genus associated with milkweeds. The larvae bore into the stems and roots, while the adults eat the leaves. The eyes are very strange in being divided, with the upper and lower sections widely separated, making in effect four eyes instead of the normal two. The antennae are ringed with white and are quite horizontal to the head.

DISTRIBUTION As a genus found throughout North America.

STERNOTOMIS VARIABILIS

COMMON NAME Variable longhorn

DESCRIPTION There are several similar, spotted, green longhorns found in the forests of tropical Africa. This species, just over 1 inch in length, is particularly common and is usually to be found on the trunks of fallen trees in forests. This female is biting a hole in the bark prior to turning and laying an egg, a common behavior in longhorns.

DISTRIBUTION Widespread in tropical Africa.

TRAGOCEPHALA VARIEGATA

COMMON NAME Variegated longhorn

DESCRIPTION The striking black and orange coloration of this spectacular longhorn is found in only slightly less brilliance in many other members of the genus, which is found in tropical Africa and Madagascar.

This species, which measures just over 1 inch, is found in tropical forests.

DISTRIBUTION Southern Africa.

OBEREA OCULATA

COMMON NAME Willow twig-borer

DESCRIPTION The slim-bodied, approximately ½-inch adults are very difficult to spot when resting on their willow foodplants in July and August. The larvae develop within the twigs. Several more similar-looking species are found in Europe, differing in only minor details from the 25 or so species from North America.

DISTRIBUTION Europe, and the British Isles.

LEAF BEETLES
Family Chrysomelidae

This is one of the largest worldwide families, with over 25,000 species. The adult beetles are normally squarely and chunkily built, often domed and tortoise-like. Almost all the known species feed on leaves. The larvae are soft-bodied and resemble slugs.

CRIOCERIS ASPARAGI

COMMON NAME Asparagus beetle

DESCRIPTION Although only about ¼ inch long, this beetle can occur in such numbers as to inflict severe damage on cultivated asparagus. The black elytra bear four whitish blotches and have red borders. Several similar species are found in Europe, all with rather variable markings. Both

larvae and adults of this species feed on asparagus, and the adults can produce quite a loud chirp.

DISTRIBUTION Widespread in Europe (including England) and northern Asia; introduced into North America.

LEPTINOTARSA DECEMLINEATA

COMMON NAME Colorado beetle

DESCRIPTION Still found feeding harmlessly on wild *Solanum* plants in its native home of the southwestern USA and Mexico, this strikingly-marked beetle has become a great pest throughout much of the northern hemisphere on cultivated potatoes. A plague of these ⅜-inch long beetles can ruin the crop.

DISTRIBUTION Spreading in many northern hemisphere countries.

DORYPHORA TESTUDO

COMMON NAME Lurid leaf beetle

DESCRIPTION At about ¾ inch, this striking species is rather larger than any European leaf beetle. It is often abundant on low vegetation where roadways run through areas of rainforest. Its bright yellow and black warning pattern gives notice of extremely noxious properties. There are several similar-looking species.

DISTRIBUTION Over much of central and tropical South America.

CHRYSOMELA POPULI

COMMON NAME Poplar leaf beetle

DESCRIPTION Poplars and willows are the foodplants of this handsome ½-inch long beetle, which is often extremely common where it occurs, for example on coastal dunes. When molested it can release a defensive liquid which reeks of carbolic acid. Several similar-looking members of the genus can do likewise.

DISTRIBUTION Across all of Europe and Asia, to Japan.

DIABROTICA sp.

COMMON NAME Flea beetle

DESCRIPTION Flea beetles are generally rather small insects which leap into the air when disturbed. About ⅕-inch long, this tropical species has been included as it illustrates the enlarged hind femora typical of flea beetles. Many species are serious pests of cultivated plants, e.g. the spotted cucumber beetle (*D. undecimpunctata*), a yellow-bodied species with seven black spots on the elytra. It damages a wide range of crop plants in North America.

DISTRIBUTION The species illustrated is from tropical America.

CASSIDA VIRIDIS

COMMON NAME Green tortoise beetle

DESCRIPTION In tortoise beetles (subfamily Cassidinae) the elytra and pronotum are extended outward to form a flattened tortoise-like carapace, beneath which the legs, head, and antennae can be retracted. This ½-inch long species lives on various mints, especially water mint, and is often found in gardens. There are numerous similar species.

DISTRIBUTION From the British Isles, eastwards to Japan.

METRIONA CLAVATA

COMMON NAME Clavate tortoise beetle

DESCRIPTION This ⅓-inch long species resembles a gall or blotch on a leaf. The edges of the pronotum and elytra are more or less transparent. It is usually found on plants of the morning glory family. Tortoise beetle larvae are strange spiky creatures which hold aloft over their backs a protective shield formed of their molted skins and droppings.

DISTRIBUTION Eastern North America and most of Mexico.

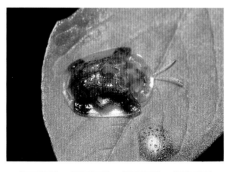

Superfamily CURCULIONOIDEA

LONG BEETLES *Family Brentidae*

The members of this 2,000-strong family are among the most bizarre of insects. The head is extremely elongated so that it is almost of a length with the equally elongated body. The antennae are often beadlike. The majority of species are found in the tropics, especially in areas of rainforest.

BRENTUS ANCHORAGO

COMMON NAME Toothpick weevil

DESCRIPTION This weird ½–1½-inch long creature can often be found in considerable numbers behind the flaking bark of dead and dying trees. This is a male, the females being much smaller and lacking the extended head. Some males are as small as the females. Long males use their snouts as lances to do battle with one another and to guard females as they lay their eggs.

DISTRIBUTION Over most of the tropical Americas; also Florida.

WEEVILS
Family Curculionidae

This is the largest family of insects, with over 40,000 known species. The head is normally prolonged into a snout or rostrum whose tip bears the jaws, the antennae being mounted about halfway along. Many species are wingless, with the elytra fused together. Most species are plant-eaters.

PHYLLOBIUS ARGENTATUS

COMMON NAME Silvered leaf weevil

DESCRIPTION The body of the ⅛–1¼-inch long weevil is covered in glinting metallic greenish scales, although these often wear off over considerable areas in older individuals. The adults are often abundant in May and June on deciduous trees. There are numerous similar-looking species.

DISTRIBUTION Europe (including the British Isles), and much of Asia.

APODERUS CORYLI

COMMON NAME Hazel leaf-rolling weevil

DESCRIPTION This ¼–⅓-inch long weevil with a rather round body and short antennae (subfamily Attelabinae) can be found sitting around on hazel leaves from May through September. The females spend many hours painstakingly rolling the leaves of hazel or birch into cradles which provide food and lodging for the larvae. The North American rose weevil (*Rhynchites bicolor*) is rather similar, but has a much longer black rostrum.

DISTRIBUTION Much of Europe, including the British Isles.

CURCULIO NUCUM

COMMON NAME Nut weevil

DESCRIPTION The ¼–⅓-inch body length of this weevil includes the very elongated snout. It is found in July and August on hazel trees, in whose nuts the larvae develop. The female gnaws into the nut with her long rostrum before laying an egg in it. The European acorn weevil (*C. glandium*) is very similar, as are several North American species with vastly longer snouts. In the larger chestnut weevil (*C. proboscideus*) from eastern North America, the snout is usually longer than the body.

DISTRIBUTION Europe (including the British Isles), and much of Asia.

CHRYSOLOPUS SPECTABILIS

COMMON NAME Captain Cook weevil

DESCRIPTION This beautiful ½-inch long weevil is normally black, decorated with a pattern of scintillating green or bluish scales. The adults are usually found sitting around on the leaves of acacia trees in dry forests. The larvae feed on acacia roots and stems, and can sometimes kill young trees.

DISTRIBUTION Australia.

OTIORHYNCHUS SULCATUS

COMMON NAME Vine weevil

DESCRIPTION This rather drab ⅓–⅜-inch long weevil is the scourge of the horticulturalist in many countries. The larvae develop on the roots of many plants and can wreak havoc in nurseries, with container-grown plants being especially susceptible. The adults are rarely seen outdoors, but often noticed walking around on an indoor windowsill.

DISTRIBUTION Almost worldwide.

INDEX

TALANTHIUM PHALANGIUM

COMMON NAME Daddy-long-legs weevil

DESCRIPTION The long gangly-legged weevils belonging to the subfamily Zygopinae are among the most peculiar members of the family. They run around on the trunks of trees in forests. The males are much larger than the females, and stand over them while they are laying their eggs in order to fend off rival males. This species mimics a harvestman (phalangid).

DISTRIBUTION Southeast Asia.

FUNGUS WEEVILS or MOLE BEETLES
Family Anthribidae

The characteristic feature of this family is the way in which the head is extended to form a short, broad, and rather blunt snout-like structure. Some species are pests of stored products, particularly coffee; most develop in dead wood. Some 2,000 species are found around the world.

MECOCERUS RHOMBEUS

COMMON NAME Fungus weevil

DESCRIPTION Most anthribids are rather drably colored in browns and grays. This African species, with its pale yellow marking, is therefore rather striking. Like many anthribids, it spends its life on tree trunks, in which the eggs are laid. Note the broad snout, which in this species bears a pair of extremely long slender antennae.

DISTRIBUTION Tropical Africa.